NATIONAL GEOGRAPHIC

READING EXPEDITIONS

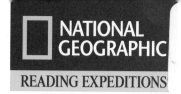

M000116073

EVERYDAY KIDS THEN AND NOW

MEXICO

PROPERTY OF
ELK MEADOWS ELEMENTARY
JORDAN SCHOOL DISTRICT

By Jean Bennett

Illustrated by Manuel Garcia

PICTURE CREDITS
3 top to bottom © Jeremy Woodhouse/Getty Images, © Royalty-Free/Corbis; 7 top to bottom © f1 online/Alamy, © Mark Lewis/Alamy; 45 left to right © Foodcollection.com/Alamy, © Bobbie Lerryn/Alamy; 46 top to bottom © Sarkis Images/Alamy, © Christian Liewig/Corbis; 48 © Kenneth Garrett.

Produced through the worldwide resources of the National Geographic Society, John M. Fahey, Jr., President and Chief Executive Officer; Gilbert M. Grosvenor, Chairman of the Board; Nina D. Hoffman, Executive Vice President and President, Books and Education Publishing Group.

PREPARED BY NATIONAL GEOGRAPHIC SCHOOL PUBLISHING
Ericka Markman, Senior Vice President and President, Children's Books and Education Publishing Group; Steve Mico, Senior Vice President, Publisher, Editorial Director; Francis Downey, Executive Editor; Richard Easby, Editorial Manager; Bea Jackson, Director of Design; Cynthia Olson, Art Director; Margaret Sidlosky, Director of Illustrations; Matt Wascavage, Manager of Publishing Services; Lisa Pergolizzi, Sean Philpotts, Production Managers, Ted Tucker, Production Specialist.

MANUFACTURING AND QUALITY CONTROL
Christopher A. Liedel, Chief Financial Officer; Phillip L. Schlosser, Director; Clifton M. Brown III, Manager.

EDITORS
Barbara Seeber, Mary Anne Wengel

BOOK DEVELOPMENT
Morrison BookWorks LLC

BOOK DESIGN
Steven Curtis Design

ART DIRECTION
Dan Banks, Project Design Company

Copyright © 2006 National Geographic Society. All rights reserved. Reproduction of the whole or any part of the contents without written permission from the publisher is prohibited. National Geographic, National Geographic School Publishing, National Geographic Reading Expeditions, and the Yellow Border are registered trademarks of the National Geographic Society.

Published by the National Geographic Society
1145 17th Street, N.W.
Washington, D.C. 20036-4688

ISBN: 0-7922-5818-5

2010 2009 2008 2007 2006
1 2 3 4 5 6 7 8 9 10 11 12 13 14 15

Contents

THEN

Ah Ik' the Beekeeper

NOW

Gloria and Luis in the Maya Water World

Ah Ik', Gloria, and Luis

The two stories in this book are connected. One story takes place long ago and the other takes place in the present. The same object becomes important in each story for different reasons. Each main character in the stories has an adventure that occurs in the same place, but thousands of years apart.

Ah Ik' the Beekeeper

This story is set in ancient Mexico in 850 A.D. Ah Ik' is a beekeeper in the Yucatán forest. He comes from a poor family. When his honey helps the village nobles, Ah Ik' becomes an unlikely hero and his adventure begins.

NOW

Gloria and Luis in the Maya Water World

Gloria and Luis live in modern Mexico. When some visitors ask their father about the location of an underground lake, the kids sense trouble. Their quick thinking saves the day and an ancient treasure.

Mexico

Mexico is a country on the continent of North America. The United States is directly north of Mexico. Mexico is about a quarter of the size of the United States. The terrain in Mexico varies from rocky deserts in the north to tropical rain forest in the south. The Yucatán is one of Mexico's peninsulas. A peninsula is a piece of land that extends into a body of water. The Yucatán is low, flat, and mostly made of limestone.

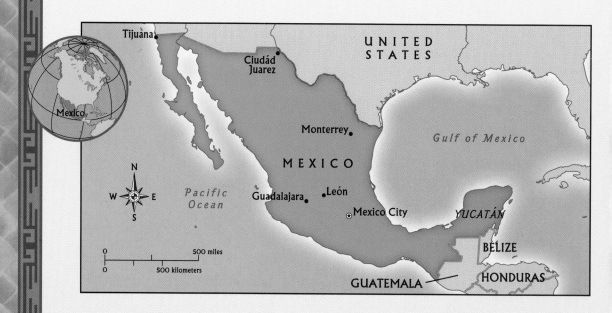

Northern Yucatán Northern Yucatán has a dry climate and low-growing plants. The limestone absorbs most of the rain that falls. Water for people and animals comes from underground lakes and wells called cenotes.

Mexico: The Facts

- Size: 756,066 square miles
- Population: 106,200,000 people
- Longest River: Rio Grande River
- Capital City: Mexico City
- Major Language: Spanish

Southern Yucatán Southern Yucatán is hot and humid. More rain falls here than in the north. In the south, the forest grows high and thick. But today, people are cutting down the forest to make room for farms.

Ah Ik' the Beekeeper

CHAPTER 1

The Sinkhole

Ah Ik' hummed softly to the bees that buzzed around their hive in the hollow tree. Several bees landed on his hands and face, but he didn't brush them away. They settled on his skin for a moment and then flew off in search of flowers.

Ah Ik' knew the busy bees would collect nectar from the flowers and bring it back to the hive. There they would make sweet honey for him to sell at the market.

Ah Ik' liked his bees. They worked hard and got angry only when they were disturbed. Ah Ik' understood that—he wouldn't like his home to be invaded by strangers either.

It was late afternoon when he began his journey home through the forest. Colorful birds flitted among the trees. He bent down and collected several brightly colored feathers, which he tucked behind his ear.

A lizard as thick as his arm went statue-still on a log when Ah Ik' walked past. Careful to avoid the sharp-edged leaves of the spiky plants, Ah Ik' moved ahead. He pushed on through the tangled growth.

Ah Ik' was almost home when the movement of a bush caught his eye. He stopped and held his breath. He wondered if it could be a deer hiding there or maybe even a jaguar. The bush moved again and he crept toward it.

As Ah Ik' came near, something leapt out at him. He clasped the small figure in his arms.

"You'll have to be much faster than that to catch me, little sister," he laughed.

"Put me down!" Ix Mix said, laughing, as she struggled out of his grasp.

"Come," Ah Ik' said. He picked up the pottery jars she'd left beside the bush. "I'll help you fetch the water."

Ix Mix followed after Ah Ik' through the undergrowth. Together they came to a cave entrance watched over by a bird with blue-green feathers and a yellow chest.

They slid down a narrow path and entered the cave. Rays of light from a hole in the roof shone on a deep, blue underground lake.

Ah Ik' asked the rain god Chac for permission to take water from the cenote, or **sinkhole.** He took the bird feathers from behind his ear and threw them into the water as a gift to Chac. He and Ix Mix filled the water jars and returned to the forest.

---

sinkhole – a deep hollow in limestone that has a pool at the bottom

Ix Mix chattered to him about her day working in the fields with their parents.

"It was hard work," she said, "but we've gathered lots of corn, beans, and squash."

"Then we should do well at the market tomorrow," Ah Ik' said. "I've got plenty of honey to sell, too."

Their mother was crouched down beside the stone-lined cooking pit when they arrived at their hut. The family sat beside the warm pit. They spread a hot mixture of vegetables and peppers onto flat circles of corn bread.

"It's good to be home," said Ah Ik'.

CHAPTER 2

Going to Market

It was still dark when Ah Ik' awoke to the sound of his mother slapping wads of corn dough to make thin bread.

Ah Ik' and his father collected their vegetables and pots of honey. His mother tied the cloth in bundles. They lifted their goods onto their backs. Loaded down, they set off for the market.

It was mid-morning when they reached the trading town. The streets were lined with people buying and selling goods. The family found a space to set out their produce to sell.

"I need to buy fish," said Ah Ik's mother.

"And salt to dry and preserve our food," his father added. He noticed a stray dog that was sniffing at their produce. "Go away!" he yelled, as he pushed the dog aside.

The dog snarled and leapt at Ah Ik's father. He shouted as the animal bit his leg. Ah Ik' shooed the dog away with a stick.

Ah Ik' inspected the wound on his father's leg. "That's a nasty bite," he said.

He reached for a jar of his honey. Carefully, he smeared the golden liquid over the injury. Then he bound a strip of cotton around his father's leg. "It will heal well."

They heard shouting at the end of the street. Men were pushing through the crowds.

"Make way for the great Xochitl Ich Ahau," they called out. "Make way for the noble lord, known as the eye of the owl."

Ah Ik' saw a richly dressed man stop at one stall to examine shells and ornaments. At another stall, he held up emerald green feathers plucked from quetzal birds. He nodded to a servant who paid the merchant.

Ah Ik's family bowed their heads as he came near their stall. Suddenly Ix Mix stepped out and held up a pot of honey to Xochitl Ich Ahau. Ah Ik' rushed forward to pull his sister back.

Instead, the nobleman reached out and dipped his finger into the honey pot. He sucked the honey from his finger and then nodded.

He spoke to Ah Ik'. "Deliver it all to my house immediately."

The nobleman moved on while his servant discussed a fair price with Ah Ik's father. Then the servant counted out valuable cacao beans in payment for the honey.

Ah Ik' gathered his pots of honey. He listened while the servant gave him directions to the nobleman's house.

"Don't wait for me to return," Ah Ik' said to his parents. "I will be home very late."

CHAPTER 3

Ah Ik's Journey

On his way to the nobleman's house, Ah Ik' stopped to watch young men playing a ball game in a yard paved with stones. The players didn't touch the heavy ball with their hands. Instead, they bounced it to each other using their elbows, knees, and hips. Sometimes they aimed the ball at a stone hoop set sideways on a wall.

One of the players called for a break, and they walked over to Ah Ik'.

"It must be hard to get the ball into that high hoop," he said to one young man.

"It is," the young man agreed. "We haven't scored a goal today. We're lucky this is only a practice."

His friend added, "If we lose a game to another team, we'll be thrown down a sinkhole as an offering to Chac."

Ah Ik' shuddered. He thought that was quite harsh. "I hope you win all of your games," he said. He went on his way.

At last he arrived at a large stone house and went to the rear entrance. There he delivered the jars of honey for Xochitl Ich Ahau.

Ah Ik' was about to leave when he noticed a monkey tied to a post. It chattered and pulled against the rope that was holding it captive. The monkey's sad eyes seemed to beg Ah Ik' to set it free. He bent down and untied the animal. Immediately it climbed into nearby trees and swung out of sight.

At that moment, Ah Ik' heard a cry behind him. He turned to see a young boy come out of the nobleman's house.

"My monkey!" he cried. "You've let him go!"

The boy's howls brought people running. The boy pointed at Ah Ik'. "He let my monkey go," he sobbed.

Servants grabbed hold of Ah Ik'. "Take him inside," one of the men ordered. "Xochitl Ich Ahau will punish him."

Ah Ik' was dragged inside the house. The servants pulled him toward a raised platform at the end of the room. He was forced down to his knees on the stone floor.

Xochitl Ich Ahau looked at Ah Ik' as though he were inspecting a bug.

"Young beekeeper," he began, "did you untie my son's monkey?"

Ah Ik' was frightened. He looked at the nobleman, swallowed, and nodded.

The nobleman's high, flat forehead creased in a frown. "The monkey belonged to my son. He was Ah Kawak's playmate." He closed his eyes. "I must think about your punishment."

Ah Ik' shook with fear. He hoped that he would not be thrown into a sinkhole as a gift to Chac like the ball players.

Xochil Ich Ahau opened his eyes and glared at Ah Ik'. "You will stay here with my son," he said. "You will be Ah Kawak's servant."

Ah Ik' sighed. His life was spared, but now he was captive, just like the pet monkey.

In the weeks that followed, Ah Ik' spent every moment of the day with his new master. Ah Kawak had been born with a weak chest. He often had trouble breathing and he tired easily.

Ah Ik' taught Ah Kawak how to play a clay flute. The child enjoyed blowing birdlike sounds and it helped him control his breathing.

Each night after the boy fell asleep, Ah Ik' wandered outside. He thought about his parents and Ix Mix. He worried that he might not ever see them again.

CHAPTER 4

The Healer

One morning Ah Kawak woke with a harsh cough. He wheezed and shook his head when Ah Ik' offered him a hot cacao drink. At midday he pushed away his favorite turkey and avocado meal.

Ah Ik' touched the boy's cheeks and forehead. He had a burning fever. Ah Ik' ran to tell Xochitl Ich Ahau and his wife that their son was ill.

"Get the village healer," the nobleman ordered a servant.

The healer arrived. He sang chants, burned incense, said prayers. He rubbed ointments and medicines on the boy's chest.

Ah Kawak's breathing eased a little, but soon his small body trembled as the fever worsened.

His mother stroked the boy's forehead and said, "What can we do?"

Ah Ik' gathered his courage. "Excuse me," Ah Ik' said. "My mother taught me how to make a drink that cures fevers."

Xochitl Ich Ahau looked at him in disbelief. Ah Kawak moaned in his mother's arms. "I'm afraid our son will die," she said.

The nobleman nodded to Ah Ik'. "Make your drink, beekeeper," he said.

Ah Ik' hurried out to the garden where he gathered some bark from a special tree. He heated a pot full of water and dropped in the bark. Then he stirred in spoonfuls of honey. He let the mixture settle.

He poured the liquid into a cup and knelt in front of Ah Kawak. His mother held the boy while Ah Ik' encouraged him to sip the sweetly scented drink. Ah Kawak continued to shiver and moan. Ah Ik' coaxed him to swallow more of the drink until it was all gone.

Slowly Ah Kawak's fever left him. It was well into the night when he finally fell into a deep and peaceful sleep.

"Thank you, beekeeper," Xochitl Ich Ahau said, and he left the room.

In the following days, Ah Kawak made a slow recovery. He rested often in his room. His mother gave him a gold bell shaped like a monkey. Whenever Ah Ik' left the boy for more than a few minutes, he'd hear the bell ringing.

Ah Ik' fed Ah Kawak fresh vegetables and fruit. He gave him spoons dripping with honey that the boy gulped down happily.

Each day Ah Ik' took him outside. He taught Ah Kawak how to whistle to the birds in the trees. The boy chased the colorful butterflies that settled on the flowers. He grew stronger and breathed more easily.

One night the nobleman called Ah Kawak and Ah Ik' outside. He pointed to the stars.

"See," he said. "The gods watch over us."

Ah Ik' looked at the glittering stars and wondered about the beings who lived in the sky.

"The movement of the stars show the time is right," the nobleman said. "Tomorrow we shall celebrate Ah Kawak's good health."

The next day, crowds of guests arrived. Many visitors wore shell jewelry and huge headdresses decorated with bird feathers. Some were dressed in animal skins.

Flutes, pipes, rattles, and singers filled the house with joyous music. Drummers pounded on hollow logs covered with the stretched skins of animals.

Ah Ik' watched Xochitl Ich Ahau dance with his wife. They faced each other and moved like tall, graceful birds.

Ah Kawak played his clay flute for the noble guests. Everyone listened and clapped at the end of the song. Then he insisted that Ah Ik' join him and together they whistled beautiful birdcalls.

When they'd finished, Xochitl Ich Ahau stood up. He put his hand on Ah Ik's shoulder.

Ah Ik's knees shook as he wondered what he had done wrong.

"Young beekeeper, you have helped my son grow strong," the nobleman said. "In return, I give you your freedom."

Ah Ik's eyes shone with tears of happiness. He stammered his thanks.

Later that night, Ah Ik' settled Ah Kawak to sleep for the last time.

The boy held his hand. "You've been a good friend," he said. He held out his gold monkey bell to Ah Ik'. "Take this. I don't need it now."

Ah Ik' left the nobleman's house at first light. He walked quickly along the streets of the town. Fruit sellers called to him, and dogs barked at his heels, but he didn't stop.

He reached the road leading to his home. He began to run faster and faster. The gold monkey bell clanged as he ran.

Ah Ik' left the road and pushed his way through the lowland forest. At last he came to the entrance of the cenote. He slid down to the waterhole. There he knelt by the underground lake. He lifted his arm, and the monkey bell rang as he tossed it into the water as a gift to the rain god, Chac.

He heard a sound nearby. Ix Mix walked into the cave entrance holding her water jars.

"Brother!" she cried. "You have come home!" She dropped the jars and ran into his arms.

Ah Ik' smiled and held her tight.

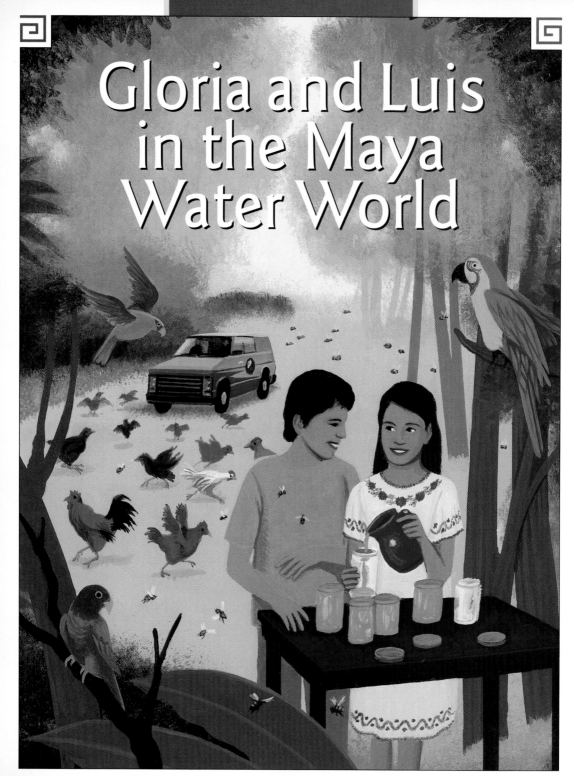

Gloria and Luis in the Maya Water World

CHAPTER 1

The Visitors

Gloria filled a jar with golden honey and tightened the lid. She laughed at something her brother, Luis, said. They were talking about traveling into town to sell the honey at the market.

Chickens clucked in the yard as they chased the grain Gloria and Luis's mother mother threw to them. A light breeze brushed Gloria's white cotton **huipil** against her legs.

Gloria looked up at the sound of a vehicle coming down the unpaved road. A mud-streaked van turned into the yard. The chickens squawked and scattered in fright.

Her father came out of their hut as the van pulled to a stop. Three men climbed from the van and walked toward him.

---

huipil – a loose embroidered garment worn by Maya women in Mexico and Central America

"*¡Hola!* Hello," one of the men called. "Are you Señor Patcanul?"

Gloria's father nodded.

"I'm Mark," the man said. "And these are my companions, Shorty and Felipe."

Gloria wondered what the men wanted. They didn't carry cameras like most visitors to whom her father showed the birds and plants of the Yucatán. He enjoyed working as a tour guide. Tourists were fascinated by his knowledge of the local wildlife and Maya traditions.

She saw Luis narrow his eyes at the strangers. She knew that he was suspicious. He glanced at Gloria and then left her side to stand beside his father.

"What brings you to my home?" Señor Patcanul asked.

"We work for the government," Mark replied. "We're mapping the underground waterholes, the cenotes, in this area."

Gloria noticed that the men all wore black T-shirts with a logo on the front. The same logo was on the side of their van.

The man called Shorty spoke. "We've heard you might know where there are unexplored cenotes hidden in the forest."

"Why does the government want to know about the cenotes?" Luis asked.

"To protect them," Shorty answered. "We dive into the sinkholes and search the underwater caves for treasures and **artifacts.**"

"Then we tell the government which cenotes need to be protected," Felipe explained.

"Won't that make it easier for robbers to know where to find the treasures?" Señor Patcanul asked. "The gifts that my Maya ancestors gave to the rain god, Chac, must not be moved or stolen."

"The government will put alarms at all important cenotes," Mark said. "The alarms will be connected to the sheriff's office."

"Do you have proof that you're from the government?" Luis asked.

"*Sí,* yes," Mark said. He went to the van and brought out a folder from which he took a letter.

---

artifact – a human-made object from a period in history

Gloria watched her father and Luis read the letter and nod to each other.

"I must think about your request," Señor Patcanul asked.

He went inside their hut. Gloria knew he would sit cross-legged on his thinking mat for some time. The family never disturbed him when he sat there.

Mark and his companions leaned against their van. Shorty unwrapped a candy bar and tossed the wrapper on the ground.

"Trash belongs in the trash can!" Luis scolded, picking up the wrapper.

It was much later when Señor Patcanul returned to the yard.

He looked at the men and frowned. "More and more people are coming to the Yucatán. I've been worried that one day the sacred cenote my father once showed me would be looted by dishonest people."

"We will safeguard its location," Felipe said.

"You are from the government," Señor Patcanul said. "I will accept your word, but you must promise not to take anything my ancestors left in the cenote."

"You have my promise," Mark said.

"Very well," Señor Patcanul said. "I will take you there in the morning. Tonight you may eat dinner with us and hang your hammocks from the trees near our hut."

That evening Gloria's mother cooked a meal of corn tortillas, beans, and a spicy salsa made with habanero chiles.

"Looks tasty, Señora," Mark said. He helped himself to the food and swallowed a large mouthful. Immediately he spluttered and his eyes watered. He gasped for breath.

Gloria gave him a glass of water. "A little hot for you, maybe?" she smiled.

CHAPTER 2

A Sacred Cave

The dawn chorus of birds woke everyone early. The divers quickly unhooked their hammocks and joined the family for breakfast.

"We've got a lot of dive gear," Mark said. "Would you kids help us carry it into the cenote for a few **pesos?**"

Luis thought for a moment. "Yes," he said. "For twenty pesos." Then he added, "Each."

Mark raised his eyebrows. "You're a sharp businessman," he said.

Gloria's mother waved to the group as they strapped on their backpacks and carted dive gear into the forest. Her father warned the men to avoid the sharp-edged leaves of the spiky plants. "*¡Beya'!* This way!" Señor Patcanul said.

----

peso – a unit of money used in Spanish America

He swung his machete and cut through the undergrowth. He led the group in a direction Gloria had never been before.

They trudged deeper into the forest and finally arrived at a place where Señor Patcanul stopped. A blue-and-green-feathered toh bird with a yellow chest flew up from a branch.

Gloria's father knelt on the ground. "I must pray for everyone's safety," he said. He spoke in a low chant for several minutes.

Then he stood up and parted the scrubby growth. "Leave your gear and follow me," he said. He slid out of sight.

Luis crawled after him. "Watch out for the snakes," he warned the men.

Gloria followed the men down through the tangled undergrowth to the stone floor of a cave. She ducked as a bat flapped overhead. When her eyesight adjusted to the dim light, she blinked in amazement at the scene before her.

Long stalactites hung from the ceiling like ancient ropes. Rays of sun from a hole above shone down on the underground lake.

Its blue-green waters gleamed like the brilliant feathers of Yucatán birds. Her father's voice echoed in the cave. "No harm will come to you," he told the men, "if you don't damage the cenote or take anything from its waters."

"Of course not," Mark reassured him.

"Now I must go," Señor Patcanul said. "I have to meet a tour group in the village."

They climbed back up the slope into the bright daylight.

"We'll help you take your gear down," Luis said to the men.

Felipe hung a tarp from the trees. He put his team's backpacks in the shade.

Gloria and Luis made several trips into the cave with dive gear, ropes, and wetsuits. The men took great care with their powerful underwater lights.

"Thanks, kids," Mark said, when the gear was in the cave. He got out his wallet and gave them each twenty pesos. "You can go home now."

Gloria and Luis returned to the forest.

"I'm staying here," Luis said. "I want to keep an eye on those guys."

"Don't you trust them?"

"Nope," her brother answered.

"Then I'll stay with you," Gloria said.

They sat behind a patch of scrub. Wild bees buzzed around them. Luis folded his arms. Gloria leaned against a rock. They waited.

The midday sun shone overhead when they heard the men come out of the cave.

"It's a real treasure trove down there!" Mark said. He opened his hand, and the sun glinted off some round, gold shapes. "What did you see, Felipe?"

"Old bones," Felipe answered. He shuddered, "And a skull."

Shorty looked pleased with himself. "What do you think of this?"

He held out a golden object and shook it. A bell rang out.

Mark grinned. "A collector will pay a fortune for that."

Gloria gasped softly. Luis put his finger to his lips to warn her to keep quiet.

The men stashed the treasures in their packs. "OK," Mark said. "Let's get down there and grab some more stuff."

"We'll clear out before the old guy comes back," Shorty said.

The divers slid back down to the cenote.

As soon as they were out of sight, Luis spoke to Gloria. "Take the shortcut out to the village and get the sheriff quickly! I'll stay here and keep watch."

"Be careful," Gloria said. She hurried away.

CHAPTER 3

Rescuing the Treasure

Luis went over to Mark's pack and took out the golden pieces. The gold was shaped into small face masks.

He opened Shorty's pack and removed the bell. He gazed at the small golden monkey. He remembered his father saying the ancient Maya believed monkeys were wise creatures. He heard a dull buzzing noise and turned around. He noticed that the old log behind him was filled with bees.

Luis smiled as he dragged the men's backpacks over. He propped them against the buzzing log.

Then he returned to his hiding place where he'd left his own backpack. He took out the beekeeping gear he always carried and packed the treasures safely inside.

About an hour later, the divers returned. They dropped bulging sacks on the ground.

"I've got a great haul," laughed Shorty. "Let's get dressed and move out." He looked for his pack and saw it beside the log. "Hey!" he said. "I didn't put my bag there."

"Me neither," said Felipe.

"Someone's been here!" Mark shouted.

Shorty spilled the contents of his bag on the ground. "The bell's gone!" he yelled.

He kicked the hollow log in anger. A furious buzzing sounded from the log.

The divers stepped back as a swarm of angry bees flew out. They crowded around the men, attracted to their yellow wetsuits. The bees landed on arms, necks, and faces.

Mark howled and tore off his wetsuit as the bees found their way inside. "Get down to the cenote!" he shouted.

The men stumbled toward the cenote, swatting and yelling. They slid down the access way followed by the furious bees.

Luis heard people coming through the bush and turned to see Gloria and his father. Following them was the sheriff and two deputies.

"Thank goodness you're alright," Gloria said. "We heard all the yelling and got worried."

"Where are the divers?" his father asked.

"Hiding in the cave," Luis said. He smiled and explained what had happened.

He showed the sheriff the men's sacks. The sheriff opened one and took out a carved ornament. "It looks like an ancient incense burner," he said. He looked into the sack. "There's enough loot in here to charge them with theft," he said.

"You can call off the bees now," Señor Patcanul said to his son.

Luis went over to his gear. He knelt beside what looked like a metal watering can. He lit a match and held it to a roll of cardboard and fabric in the can. Then he covered the can with a lid. He moved an attached flap in and out to fan the fire. Smoke rose from the spout. He threw a net veil over his head and took his bee smoker to the cave entrance.

"Come out!" he called to the men. "I'll settle the bees!"

The divers scrambled up, batting at the bees that buzzed around them.

"Get them off!" yelled Mark.

Gloria watched Luis hold his bee smoker near the bees. The angry buzzing gradually eased. Luis walked toward the hollow log. The bees followed him back to the log.

"Well done," his father said.

The sheriff arrested the badly stung divers. His deputies collected the sacks of stolen treasures from the ground.

Luis went to his pack and took out the monkey bell and the golden masks. He held them, not wanting to part with the link to his ancestors. Finally he turned and gave the treasures to the sheriff.

"What will happen to them?" Luis asked.

"I know a team of scientists and trustworthy cenote divers," the sheriff said. "I'll have them contact you, so you can supervise the return of the artifacts."

CHAPTER 4

Giving Back to Chac

That weekend, Señor Patcanul led new divers to the cenote. This time, the team was a group of scientists from the university.

"Phew!" Gloria said as she struggled with a large pack. "You've got a lot more gear than the looters had."

"You'll soon see why," said one of the team members, smiling.

At the cave entrance, Gloria's father knelt down. He said prayers of thanks for the return of the treasures to the cenote.

Some of the team put on their wetsuits. One diver carried a large, oblong box.

"What's that?" Luis asked.

"It's an underwater video camera," he said.

Gloria and Luis watched the team disappear into the underground cave.

"One day I'll be a diver," Luis said. "Then I'll see the cenotes of our people."

"Me too," agreed Gloria.

A few of the team members remained above ground. Gloria and Luis were surprised to see a woman unzip a padded bag and take out a television screen.

"Television won't work here," Gloria said.

"This is much more interesting," said the woman. "Come and see."

Gloria and Luis sat in front of the screen while the woman worked a control panel.

"It shows what the video camera is filming," she explained. "Look!"

"Wow!" Gloria gasped. A diver appeared on the screen. He wore a mask and flippers and had dive tanks strapped to his back. "He's under the water!"

A trail of bubbles rose from the diver. He swam through the cenote, kicking his legs to move forward in the water.

Other divers came into view. One of them turned toward the camera and raised her hand. She held the golden monkey bell.

Gloria and Luis watched as the diver glided toward an underwater cave. Her flashlight lit up the submerged stalactites. Carefully she placed the bell on a ledge. She stayed there for a moment, hand outstretched and swaying gently in the water.

"Thank you," Gloria whispered. "Chac's gift is safely home."

Mexico Then and Now

Beekeeping Then The ancient Maya kept bees that were native to the Yucatán. The Maya believed that the bees were linked with the spirit world. Each hive of bees produced a few pounds of honey every year.

Beekeeping Now Today, most beekeepers in the Yucatán use African bees. These bees make much more honey and are easier to keep than the native bees. The ancient tradition of beekeeping with native bees is dying out and so are the bees.

A beekeeper cleans a honey frame.

Sports Then A popular ancient Maya game used a rubber ball and a hoop. Many historians believe this was the first team sport. The winning team was praised and rewarded. The losers were often killed.

Sports Now Today, the most popular sport for the Mexican people is soccer. Many people play soccer every day. People also enjoy going to watch professional soccer teams play.

Write a Compare-and-Contrast Essay

Think about the characters in the stories of Ah Ik' and Gloria and Luis. How is your life similar to and different from theirs?

- Choose one of the characters, Ah Ik', Gloria, or Luis.

- Copy the Venn diagram below into your notebook.

- Use the diagram to show how your life is similar to and different from the character you chose.

- Use the example of Ah Ik' below to get started.

- Write a one-page compare-and-contrast essay about how your life is similar to and different from the character.

Ah Ik'

Me

Keeps bees

Both like to help people

Go to school

Read More About Mexico

Find and read more books about Mexico. As you read, think about these questions. They will help you understand more about this topic.

- What types of food did people eat in ancient Mexico?

- What sorts of jobs did people have in ancient Mexico?

- What are some of the customs of the people of ancient Mexico?

- What is the culture like today for the people of Mexico?

SUGGESTED READING
Reading Expeditions
Civilizations Past to Present: Mexico